In Daily Accord
FRANK GOLDEN

salmonpoetry

Published in 2008 by
Salmon Poetry,
Cliffs of Moher, County Clare, Ireland
Website: www.salmonpoetry.com
Email: info@salmonpoetry.com

ISBN 978-1-903392-75-1

Cover artwork: *Elsewhere Series 2* by Hazel Walker
Cover design & typesetting: Siobhán Hutson

For the three women who figure –
Berry, Eve and Josie (1922-2007)

Acknowledgements

Particular thanks go to Hazel Walker for her permission to use her painting ELSEWHERE – SERIES 2 and to Pat Laheen, Mary O'Malley, Valerie Whelan, David Donohue, Mark Kilroy, John O'Reilly, for reading and commenting on the text.

Some of these poems appeared in a broadsheet distributed by the Clare Champion as part of the Clare Poetry Collective.

Special thanks to Jessie Lendennie and Siobhán Hutson at Salmon for their care and imaginative presentation of *In Daily Accord*.

On the 16th of May 2003 I began composing a number of short poems on a daily basis and continued this practice until February 2005. I had done something similar a decade earlier, accomplishing daily drawings in tandem with poems.

The poems or shorts are 2, 3, and occasionally 4 lines in length and are loosely based on Haiku and Senryu forms. As with anything done on a daily basis over such a length of time, certain voices, personalities, locales and dramas play themselves out. Some of the poems are italicised indicating a voice other than the narrating I of the collection. *In Daily Accord* is essentially a collection of word stills recording the present.

Frank Golden
January 2008

May

The most casual of days
Constructing the template of memory
The bathwater overflowing

Scent of fresh lemon balm on my fingers
Rose nettle tips at my feet
The comfort and unity of striving things

Two swallows
Above a barking dog
Equals

Sublime birdsong
Inundates
The roofless mill

Lakewaterlightening
O
My completing life

Bell thock to throng
The funeral spine
Remorseless river

Light forms from our dead
We remove to a leafless world
Transparently

Crow sky falling
The four bridge portals at Golden
Open to the dead

Slip into this
Life River Death
Always fall to your deepest kiss

We drive westwards
Into the swollen land
Our dreams behind us

Some lives never rise
The mind illuminates
No anchoring space

To start with understanding
The predicate of love
The desire to imagine an end

We sit to each other's eyes
Bleeding
As the light degrades

A moment
Songs in the wild trees thrive
Loves present to their love surrender

In a love that does not fully contain us
Undelivered by the graciousness of being
Daylight takes on an indifferent sureness

Years of deep intent
Constructing patterns
Something to penetrate later

The piano in mud
Is larger than the human body
And more emotional

We peer walk sing
Green sky
Grinding moon

I'll stay with you
It's easier
But nothing is permanent

I remark on each bird in turn
Bullfinch stonechat swan
Yellowhammer blackbird sparrow

No one stays longer than they must
We outlast to our own needs
Outlandishly determined

To know rain
To leaf–ululate
Its runnel kiss

Dark the rain
In the dark stream
And overhanging trees

I might as well kneel
It's a form of prayer
Trying to hear

Plunged into darkness
The day stays
Beneath my feet

No nothing else
I have enough
It would only be wasted

Lovers stride the chill beach
A thick blanket limply sausaged
Surely it's too cold

Sometimes we fall
She tells me
How deterred she is

Sacral strange dreams
Lawnmowers delving
Through pre-mown channels

Walking to an unknown address
To an uncoordinated rendezvous
In an uncertain and undetermined life

Pool tables stuffed into car boots
Coffee tables trounced by saws
Lovers doing what they do best

Starling and swallow song
Channels of my lovers flesh
Jet pool of ecstatic eyes

Scent of mild screams
Stems of darkening Acquilegia
The mysteriously known and unknown

Your touch
Faint life of clouds
Rustling seed pods

She plaits my back in soap
She showers me down
She ferrets between my legs

No song today
We ate and spoke
Of unexpected endings

She remembers
How green was the first day
How dark it became

She gnaws on carrot sticks
To soothe her stemming teeth
Furious with growth

She eats buttercups
She speckles her legs with petals
She pisses in the long grass

My ducks taken by the fox
My tomatoes diseased and dying
Only my potatoes growing like women

Bluebells from Ballyhannon
Two gold starred porcelain cups
A white dog barking in the dark

Surprise the bones in my throat
Kiss me to what you know
In the flesh

The facile argument doused then re-ignited
The difficult real argument
Smouldering elsewhere

I work like a horse
I eat like one
I'm fat and I can't locate my future

June

An outstanding woman
Planting strawberries
Instead of the past

Starling song in the wind-leafed beech
Pegged garments on the ash line blown

The wind dies away then the rain
Our palms press so
We kiss to what we know

Thinking of how I want to remember the present
I ask her to go into the garden
And assemble herself fleetingly

Dream of a small girl
Glossy blond ringlets
Easing out her tiny dead baby

The green baize of a dark room
The plaid curtain billowing inwards
Onto dry books and my body

She longs for her body to be a relic of her life
She is impatient both to live and to be dead
Her refuge is the fire she still feels

I stand and mentally join the parts
I see
What is apparent is also luminous

I hold her baby
I hold her baby
I hold her baby

My daughter plants sweet peas
On a brilliant evening in June
She grows

                        Mowed
                        Colander rain
                        My dry skull

        In flow
        Our solar lives
        In time

                        That sea
                        This bog
                        These sheep

        Curved window
        Clotted garden
        Spooled in rain

After days away
My daughter
Simply hugs me

Petrified blooms
Of my bookish intent
All that waived life

Beyond protocol
Lightness
When an old one dies

Second born
Sturdy as a door
Caught dreaming her transit

Age becomes more abstract
Rain falls
Seams of buttercups waver

Carry the coffin in bleak heat
Midges swarming over
Our darkening grief

The path meanders
In the fogged distance mother blurs
Synapse by synapse

My arms beneath her breasts
We shuffle to the toilet
Both crutch and beast

She falls by the washstand
We pitter patter back to bed
Her eyes water a little and then clear

She doesn't mince her words
I'll miss you she says
As I cut the brambles from about the quince

A slight rain
Falling on fennel fronds
She unwavering

In the whole quiet of evening
Bird flight through shadows
Clear shape of their song

Although I wasn't there
I believe it happened
Though all reports describe it differently

No not gone
The light though changed
Is still strong

Blue sky   white rocket flowers
Gold cat asleep amongst a settlement of stones
Grumbling sound of dishes being scolded

Still buttercups
Scent of lavender
Transposed halcyon

Heart breaking
Ease of rain
You fall on me

Here at the end of the world
We suddenly believe a storm-pressaging darkness
Will overwhelm our faith

Flies gather in the evening dusk
An unresolved couple try to burn
A tiered mound of branches

She touches his bottom
He opens the newspaper

Not listening not hearing
Voices subsiding
The humid night darkening

Ivy fudges the quartered glass
Of the old Parochial House
Dimming its testament of light

Love –
Affirmed love
No savage ideals

The tongue always
Seeks its object
Bread or cunt

Without
Without one
To touch

Pedestrian
I walk in clichés
Impoverishing

July

We prove we have the capacity
Even in suddenly drear light
To touch each other

Called to HELP
I ease him naked
To a sitting position

By violet descent
I lean over her
Seeking nectar

Organic eggs
Smell of her
Active on my fingers

No bleeding hands
No trees in flower
No suppliant arms upraised

The air sours
Moths flounder on my face
Night's bulging chaos

My throat is wrong
It weakens me

From afar I see her
My hands flower
My earth dampens

A china dog shatters
The TV turns blue
In an adjoining room

The baby dips
Its pink finger
Into the spider nest

Legs that wont let me down
Clouds that will not rain
Ascensions that will complete

Never before
To have had a focused vision
Or to have wanted to live

10.48 pm
Root-sopping rain
Drenched potato flowers

Tonight
I accept
What is offered

I sit
Not wishing to fail
My darkness

Emotional
I stop to piss on the long road home
Hazard lights blinking

Asked to name my life in metaphor
I imagine an atomic mushroom cloud
Slow expansion   its shadowing dominion

Actions
Consequential words
Images are what we store

I change her knickers
I comb her hair
We talk of the past

Mackerel
New spuds
Rain   butter

Worship of the day
Routines of chat
Fluent faithful evenings

In the supermarket carpark
E repeats the oracle of Delphi's
Succinct prophecy

August

Black bathing suit
Her green eyes and strong hair
Her wet body   her breasts

She slept in cold anger
She woke silent and grave

Bolting lettuce
Wilting potato stems
Seething dreams

O2 blue sky
Swallows gathering
Still

White bed
Sex
Nullity

Write something nice
Say something interesting
Love me

Lost at the beginning of the day
And lost at its end
These are my desperate symmetries

Sleeping with a woman in a room
Ceilinged in historic maps
A dressing gown in 2 pinks ghosting on the door

I can absorb
I can reverse positions
I can be adept

The two ladies of Llagollen
Embossed leathers   totemic wood
And a short intricate bed

An evening of Socratic dialogue
Provençal duck spatula diced broccoli and cauliflower
Wine onion sauce and pesto

The darkest nights flower dreams of tongues
Eased into the hole
Slugging terrible excrescences and betrayal

Hold fast the ground is moving
The day overwhelming
The cry cried and lost

Take a dark tongue
Cut it into unspeakable shapes
Dry flour and fry

Sadness is one thing that
Restricts the expansion of a life
Meanness another

Carrying the Pollock
Along Murioch strand
Being overwhelmed

My pink shirt on the bedstead
My lover beside me
Bleeding

In this house of clocks
No time to dwell
On what is hastening

Hand on my thigh
The excited dog
Beneath the bed

I lick the place
I imagine its body
And its grace

He doesn't know
When it will happen
Only that it will

Burning
To reveal
That I burn

She leaves   waving
The sky clouded over
Nasturtiums averted

There always comes a stage when I resent
A lover's easy laughter
When contentment in others distorts me

She says her sister is scum
She cleans her shitty bed
She picks broken glass from her arm

Sleep here
Love me
Make no noise

You look cherishable
You look like more
Than I ought to possess

A farmers tan he says
Just like chicken
The white meat is best

You'd be happier with someone else
Someone to wake with in your own parish

September

I remember how you stood
Your brown body brimming in water
Your flounce of curls against the sun

Lover where are you
Distancing
Remembering someone else

The jealousies
We are prone to
The shadows we dwell in

Things rectify
Audacities balanced
Sweet acts retrieve us

I take my lover's call
I snap discolouring leaves
I poke my boot in raw ash

Inelegant deception
Flamboyant suspicions
Translations of the other

Your eyes flooded with tears
Your disconnection from me
The act that binds us makes us smaller

She sits in the rear of the car
She counts the money
Realizing what she has sold she cries

Things change
The light darkens
What was loved becomes reproachable

Image of buildings burning
He was my hero she says
Now he's everyone's

The toilet roll on the edge of the table
The newspaper highlighting suicides at the cliffs

The assurances love brings
Its pact of bliss
The dark insights it thieves

Standing in sun
Face flowering
A bee surges my nose

Listening to the hem split
Wind about the outline
Of our shared act

September fire
Eating peaches and mint ice-cream
Leaning into our change

My daughter has rituals to do
Witchings in the orchard
Clouds to uphold

Midnight – a dog barks
The electric blanket
Weakens my thighs

The fire dies
I call mother
I think of breakfast

Drunk
Alone
The TV alarms me

I brush my teeth
I fill a pint glass with water
I turn the blanket off

On a dark pier in an ebbing tide
Our querulous voices
Retreat from the brink

Lean into this wind
Call out a mission love
Dedicate your life

We talk but it doesn't lighten us
Nothing left to advert to
Nothing but a leaden history

Mother I watch for discrepancies
How you look when you say
The voices are on again

It's not that it's impossible
To imagine it ending
Or to believe I would feel nothing

Stars are burning
I eat you

Love
Tightening and loosening its hand
Our intricate and unfinished possibilities

I await the unfastened light
Your smile will spill

Impatient to collate
I pick through
What I have defined

Silhouette of trees
Chunks of stone
Fragrance of stars

Desire
The comfort of holding
What was lost

When your hands grow old
And the tray is brought
Will you curse your carers

October

Too hot
The bed alive

Did you sleep with her?
Fire! Fire!

Skull fuck
Womb fuck
Ass fuck

Take this
I don't need it anymore

Your disquieting silence
Be generous
Sleep in my arms

Her pink sweater
Her breasts
Her blush

The beach at Keel
The fishermen gutting bass
The rock we pissed in

We can't go back now
Our bodies have changed

Free to say to one key person
That paying a high price for what you want
Is just part of the deal

Forty of us in a line
Before the sea
Clipboards stopwatches action

I know
I once wanted it
But these things pass

Let me see
There's not much left
But I'll try

For this lack of attention I punch you
For standing and not touching me
I punch you

Draw close
Hammer my lips
Suck out my tongue

You avert your eyes
Your lips
You step aside

Obedience and
Professional attentiveness
Isn't everything

Hold me
Be generous
Extend yourself

They come in dreams
The gatherers
Wading through water

Marry me
Cook for me
Kiss   Kiss   Kiss

It is my body
That states my faith
In you

Nine times out of ten
I will lift the feather
And remark on its perfection

November

November rain storm
Running to save my life
The washing stippled with burrs

Walked the mountain this way
Placed a stone from Keel Beach
In the elbow of a bough

Wounded though I feel no pain
In need of attention
Though I do not bleed

In my mother's house
Every room
Leaks music from the past

Stand here
Say whatever it is you feel
Don't   don't hold back

Light that is not constant
Love which is obvious

Drunk – sopping crumbs
Of almond and orange blossom cake
Johnny Cash parched in the background

At eighteen her body swerves achingly close
She claims her ground or is it mine
Standing in her puff-pink top and jeans

He says she has to apologize first
For breaking his windows and putting glue in the locks
She could have gotten off easy but not now

Overlooking the sea
Eating pumpkin seed buns
Talking of Francis   Isuelt and the war

Midnight protection
The car door frozen
My lover upstairs awaiting song

Cutting up a body
Putting it in a bucket
Thrill of morningsong

What would you like
Her tongue
Her fingers

Where to locate meaning
I rise I cook I launder
The days shorten

Moriarty's hair takes him to Upanishads
To awakenings avalanches depths hells heights
To the removal of Psyche's blind and to the open window

Chesnut and red lentil soup
Ham hocks and clementine cake
Pears Belle Helene and cream

December

The Rhine's shape has shifted
Though I still echo here
Ghosts walk with me

He had nothing
Had never been recognized
His only luxury was sex

Life
Complete the full course
For expiry date refer to flap

My decrepitude
My inarticulateness
My inescapable beautiful inadequacy

Passion and the pregnant woman
Second trimester sex
The Dr Ruth fuck on the edge of the bed

To look at this
And feel nothing

Full moon
Even the house leek leaning
Catching the rays

Instinct and intelligence
The nebula of one in the other
What we know of what matters

Falling in snow
Whole fields of earth

No faith in the rightness of the male
No joy in the softness of the female
Only danger between them and despair

A saner man might have looked more alienated
Sadam's eyes locked on the universe in waiting
Locked in his universe waiting

I am emotional she says
I cannot say these things discretely
Stop fucking her Can't you stop fucking her

Driving along a highway
The sudden panic that a tunnel brings
The desperate need to exit   consult a doctor and sleep

We arrive home at dusk
Light candles
Mix the pudding and wish

Dishes cleared away
Whiskey returned to the cupboard
Brimming stockings laid before the fire

Beautiful sex
Walk in rainfall
Day widening to stillness

Rain
Your hand in mine
Through darkness

Drive carefully she says
I love you
I really love you

Hold still
Stick your finger in
Wait

Your turn will come
The moment you wait for
Believe it or not

I was really hurt
When you didn't come
All I could hear was the rain

January

The year begun
In a walk
Through bog

Take it if you want it
It's what I offer
Restrictions and all

Fine
Take it
If that's what you really want

Voice defeating voice
The night ugly and chaotic
My dreams tortured and frayed

I listen for how their words stain
How something unclean and despairing
Festers and expands

Companionable warmth between us
We ate boiled ham
Cabbage and potatoes

No one is called twice
What is relinquished fades
Love or gifted ways it is all the same

Winter night
No woman
But it's alright

By Gregan's
In light snow
A russet fox steals west

Contours of flesh
Rolling vistas
Cries diminishment sleep

Bind me to oak
Let my leaf-tongue sun
Bludgeon me

Always this bed
Words such as these
My untouched body

It is her tears I remember
Was it her sadness I craved
Was that how I prolonged my interest

Yes I can describe the act
Its poignancy
Its fatedness

He vanished
Into small scenes
From the past

Some day I will ask
What the circumstances were

Agree with me
As a sign
We are possible

Blanket off
Alarm set
Awaiting snow

There are always those
Who will speak the harsh truth
Brilliantly

February

I trawl through my anger
Repeating phrases   accusations
Perfecting my reduction of her

The wind blows
Strong enough you would think
To strip us of what is dead

Call everyone
I have an answer
I understand

Night full of stars
Moon-washing in the orchard
Cold shadows of trees

Be absorbed by me
Let us have difficulties
Which are ours alone

She wanted to see her diseased ovary
Not to touch it just to draw it
To come to know it as an object like a chair or bed

Sun on Cappanawalla
Lavender cloud
White Blackthorn blossoms

Brent geese on the north shore
Deep footprints on the curve of Rhine
Sun behind the mountain by 5

Digging in spring
Stones disclosed
And cleared

I stroke her hair
Lifting it away from the bowl
As she vomits

Odalisque
Nipples navel cunt
The zest to fuck each other

She says his penis is broken and redwings are infrequent visitors
And that some days you just want to turn everything off
And run screaming from the building

His father crept into his bed at nine
30 years later his life in ruins
He called a conference of the family

I will see you yet
Admit to your failure
Ill mothering the past

March

I lay in bed for months
The sky became intolerable
I fell down before it and could not rise

His pain
His fear
His desire solely for repose

I want to close my eyes
I have no appetite no ambition for anything
I want to die

Last supper
My mother's body
Her blood in the commode

No fear
Night gathers
Day will follow

Orchard daffodils on the table
Blooming forsythia in the rockery
Washing blown dry in the sun

Love
Money
What Comes Between

Eight pink tulips resting in my palm
And if one pink tulip should accidentally fall
Across your breast between your legs let it lie there

No lover in her bed
In lieu of the priapic she lusts in grass
Sweet systems of the sky attend her

Mid-night in March
A little grass a willing mate
Becoming frenzied profligate

The day was wet
I did not write
Or truly speak

Mother in her shit
Crawling on the floor
Unable to make it to the light or bed

Recidivism
The sex patterns in our brains
No blue sky revokes

Inside the virtue of your lust
I night my bones

It isn't always enough
To talk to you
To know where you are

Spring again
Thickening
Simplifying

Let's keep it simple
Sit down next to me
How clean are you

Miracle
That a man will come
Who needs and wants me for who I am

I gather seaweed
In Polish coal bags
A paradoxical environmentalist

Coffined
Underneath
A Wellness Centre

He speaks of alienation,
What he wants for himself
Is a kind of freedom

To flee family and friends
Drink to excess in a
Southern place and paint

May my daughter look on me in imploded old age
The clear structure of my bones visible
A quick death imminent

Estrangement
Imagining the other
Renunciations in absence mount

April

2am
A single moth at my lightless window
I am flame to something

Living through air
Falling and in the falling
Living

We sit together for hours
He heals computers
No gold altars no candles or oil

He thinks he can walk away from it
The complex difficult life that absorbs him
He thinks he can walk away

The exterior freedom he imagines
The interior freedom he deserves
The love he imagines might simplify him

After death comes attentiveness to life
To presences and voices
To the incidence of magic

It never ends as you think it will
Argument or resolution

One man's obsession with Rapunzel
Gives way to another's feeling for Cinderella
I dream of the woodcutter and deliverance

Midnight
Sole of my footmate
Warm and soft

A friend suggests apology
There is a strength she says
In judicious capitulation

The obscene cynicism
And depravity of power
Our useless rage

The dead scattered and twisted
In sacrifice eulogised
For this dark continuum

In the hillside wood
Trees have fallen
And in my heart

Miss what
You
Less

Write
Seed
Relinquish

I bake rum cake
Drink most of it
Iron awkward shirts

Is this the day
Will it happen now
Will I say what I need to

May

Rain has come at last
To the orchard
We depart without distortion

She would say it
Out of boredom from distrust
Call you banal intransigent defeatist

She could seduce any of us
On the way to the toilet

Making love just past mid-day
May showers   glabrous leaves
Pearl sprays of apple blossom strengthening

Through drink
Might we cobble peace
And stupefied contritions

Have we dwindled to this
Abstract presences
Lives held in check for auspicious futures

I weed
I talk
I resolve

We can still talk
Through the night
Implying accusing resisting loving

I stop on the mountain road and sleep
The dead gum in my hand
Still tacky when I wake

J came ate rice and white chocolate
And recalled stopping a tractor
With his bare hands in a harrowed field

Her body reminded me of a thickening pig
One that needed to be released in the foothills
And chased mercilessly to the sound of horns

It was a good day for some
Others were raped
Or heard their children cry and were powerless

Her faith in love
In its unconditional persistence is gone
Without love she is lost

He will go to a small island
Sit on a barstool order the best local wine
Pour a glass settle his back against the counter and Gaze

While writing crap a swallow entered
Was taken by the cat and eaten
Its shit is by the telephone

Think of this
As a moment
Already forgotten

Day of days love-making
Your woman with child
Picnic on the land of your dreams

The blood may be bearing down
As you say
But I cannot taste it

Why would you say that
Knowing the conversations we've had
How protective I am   Given what I demand

June

No blind emotion
Only attachments and curiosity
As to what is missing

The past
Present
And how

Full moon – the well water bottled
My witching daughter
Luminous by snails

Tell everyone I love them
I'm dying   Am I dead
Can you feel my pulse

Oughtmama valley
Beautiful
As breasts or thighs

When I no longer sang
I thought I would sing again
Though I never did

The fire spends itself
You begin to walk
Walking becomes a duty

Today Mother enjoyed the idea that she might die during
the radio Mass from Roscommon   but she didn't
Instead she ate vanilla Vienetta topped with Satsuma
segments and cream
a McVities chocolate biscuit melting in her fingers
which she sucked

Today I told mother
You've led a good life. You've been a good mother.
    We love you.
She looked at me   *We love you too* she said

Mother hallucinates   Her hearing is bad
When did you start talking to yourself she asks
I didn't I say I'm not

I own a fourteenth century castle
Simplicity and elegance
I'm an ideas man   money simply accrues

Love is acknowledgement
She wraps her arms around me
Thank you for everything

Fifteen years ago a stiff south westerly blew me down the hill
from John Irwin's to the Pinnacle well
Today the wind like memory was in my face
I cycled and almost fell into the throes of roses screaming
    from the ditch

Cleaning the commode
Pasting Sudocreme on her open sores
Rub my back she pleads *Rub my back*

She kisses hard
The woman I love
She's honest and she kisses hard

Nothing commends us like love
Love simplifies life
It makes us possible

Walking full tilt in moonlight
Frittered flight of bats
Stone repose of night-time cows

July

Gone again
The one I'm closest to
Can you hear this

There's a blue moon coming
Like the promise of something strong
A doubling of something graceful that might ease

With you without regret
House to the slope of the mountain
My back to your breast

I know time is short
There is only one thing I want to say
Are you listening

Angels entered her denser parts she said
I wondered where those were

There's a boy I like she said
The lake   his hair   his eyes
As a rule long-haired boys aren't gay are they

Famously she cried
Love is a decision

Everyday I ask
Is it gone
Love of a shared destiny

Men on imaginary telephones
Men simulating fucking
Men hugging and kissing me

Arguing every step of the way
Around the Flaggy Shore
A beautiful sunset ruined

Only cows privy to my screams
The sea in rain
Fields in bloom

Burnt out
White star
Would I were

'Front Crawl'
That was as far as we got
Though we made a baby

No deliberate act of hatred
Just gradual antipathy
The ardent made soft

Call me
Love me
Offer me the truth

To know what is required
Not of yourself
But of others

Intricate needs
Ten hours of other people
O to be a duck

Burnt out on being
Excessed on excess
Solitude as a wish

Take him to a prostitute
Teach him to masturbate
Might that quell his pain

August

How's the head   Do voices assail you
Do you crave to smell that woman's arse
Are you compelled   Tell me if you can

We seek worms
Spraying detergent on the lawn
Waiting for the toxic pool to flush them out

The autist casts
And hooks a tree
Under a mackerel sky

Not the bed itself
Just a desire to be close
Rolls her

The effort to negate the reactive
To load ones touch
To exquisite the other

The storm tore limbs from trees
Uprooted sunflowers and delphiniums
Some days are metaphors for love

Then I came
Broken fingernails
Burning Burning

I smooth her hair
Desired or undesired
As an assault on time

There is a simpler life she says
There is a middle way
Complications can be avoided

Some days end badly
That is their destiny

Not loving is a kind of cripplehood
I would stand differently
If I could

August rain
The table cleared
The swollen river threatening

Stars and the single man
The river and its bridge
Silence on the road towards moonlight

To reach the bottom is always difficult
Even in clear water
Breath by breath you realise

She removes her jeans her top
And stands
Moving her hips

My guilt is my meanness
If I could love wholly
That to my capacity

As she came out of the toilet
She looked like a woman
I might desire objectively

Tomorrow is another 1st day
Her new uniform
The absence of boys

September

Looking at photos
It appears
We might have been happy

She cries
We'll fight on she says
And cries more deeply

My father photographed Churchill
Survived the war
Grew roses like beautiful atrocities

In Q
Ironing curtains
Listening to Russian

I touch her bottom in greeting
Don't touch me like that
Kiss me like this

One breath
All that is given

Soft hands   strong legs
All that you need
In a man

Use your hand
Beat me
Let me know how it feels

It's life
Nothing in front
Nothing behind

Ankle deep in turnips
Liquid clouds falling
Violet light inviolate day

From her cell-cloud fingers – lightenings
In delicious obedience I perish
Slave to my whispered name

His embrace
Moved
My stool

He wanted to steal away
And breathe before anyone awoke
He wanted to relieve his absorbed breath

This much I can stand
This much and no more

Were it to end
I don't know what I would do
I would swim out

All my hungers
Beloved Beloved
Mouth to mouth

Longing for death but eating well
Still checking the mirror
Still commenting on her hair

It's hard work dying
Worse than the most routine labour
Harder even than loving without passion

A curlew on the rock near Parkmore
Tide collaring the narrow causeway

Picking Berries on the road to Aughinish
Stillness of the highest tide this season

The wind blows chive minarets
My lover calls
And I waver

Animals
That's all we are
Animals

October

Fois Gras
Lemoncello
Cigarettes and booze

Night rain
I touch my lover's breasts
And dance

No family   no home
No demanding love
Only my goals as darlings

The garden is ready for winter
I seal window frames and doors
I write to my lover poems in decay

Contained aloneness
Contradiction of togetherness
Consolation of absence

To think that I might tolerate
Anyone always
In battle and blood

Those guys fucking with the prisoners
They're not us
They're not real Americans

The fat lady in the bank
Talks and talks and talks
To the fat teller

Reckless breath
You again
Upon my mouth

Bodies
In possession
Of the bed

He walks across an entire room
He touches the young man he desires

A stranger greets me in a strange town
Appallingly he asks me
How's she cuttin' Frank   how's she cuttin

Finally we were meticulous
In not saying anything at all

She saw the man's leg explode
Her own body drench in glass
The police came later and dispensed valium

A small act
We begin again
Lighter than before

I drive to drive
The sun ablaze sinks
The lighthouse undeterred lights

The terror of moonlight
And insatiable women

Such trees
Such a sky
Nights' ormolous moon

No
One
Turns
One
On

I knew from the beginning
That night would come
And I would offer myself

November

At three o clock in the morning
I was reminded that the floor
Of our house was unclean

In middle life
Kisses reverse
Your thoughts

The window with its pendant amber heart
Lockets the drear light of winter

WAR
WAR
WAR

Breath Life
To believe in and desire
What is offered

We walked on
Stars of our perished past
Gleaming

There'll be a car waiting and a room
There'll be an initial destination
But nothing more

As though I had woken with the thought
That this was not the life
I was destined to inhabit

Today I made three things
Poem   dinner   chutney
Carefully

Daily trauma of confused emotion
Acceptance of the body
Relief of the sea

I wanted
What was inside
Mined out

Watching live TV in a Cammargue B&B
Cups of Laphroaigh in hand
The smell of nail varnish remover still reeking from her knickers

Petrach said
Avignon was the foulest place
In Christendom

Late afternoon
Overlooking the square in Vaison de la Romaine
The Tobacconists' neon wobbles then grounds the
    eastern corner

Aching we strive to move beyond the bed
The market below assembles routinely
Pruned plane trees unsettle my stomach

Not you face
Not your body
Not your life

O Love
O Deceit
Turning

What you turn towards when you turn away
Knowledge of the love
You offer or negate

Life or the Work as ends
She could have slept with him
Asshole of great art

We watch the light change
We make love
Some acts determine time

December

Mid-winter pink
Sea purpling to mid-bay
Kitsch

I bite my nails   I remember my dreams
I tell my truth
Outlandish though it seems

In the evening
He was quite content
To tend the fire

The thought of her on her knees
The room imperfect
The curtains sucked outwards

It was a matter of pride
So he ate alone
And bothered no one

There is no other way
I know that
Do you feel the same

Extremes
The ivied gutters
Breaking under rain

Seductions are often imperfect
I remember how dramatic you were that night
Like furniture tumbling downstairs

This is your last chance
Tell her life is insane
Linger if she steps back

She is as necessary as the sea to me
Side by side we are genuine and true

A wind that would make you pity nature
That would make you want to open your doors
And gather saplings and bushes about the fire

I used to see Volcanoes burning   trees aflame
And now
Less

I thought
I had an answer
But I was wrong

Smell of snuffed candles
Stockings filled and hung
Orange roses opening quietly

Left-over pudding put aside
Hot water bottles
Offered to the guests

No more whiskey tonight Frank
That's it

Men and women
The uncertainty principle
No unified theory in fact

Listen for what divides us
What we thought was in the mind
Was in the heart

What do birds hope for
The shore to appear
Food to be ample in winter

January

In silence bones coming down
The grisly dead hunted and found

Weeping for his children rotting under mud
The days are brutal
And they merge

Our traipse through life
The immateriality of appearances
Our acclaim of objects

I tell the child the aluminium mice eat aluminium to keep
    their bodies bright
When she disbelieves I tell her that it's contact human
contact that intensifies their glow
Momentarily she appears un-nerved   confounded
As though some
wearying misalliance of truth and sham must be unalloyed

Just when you think its over it begins again
Cherished things fall
So I gather them

Women you thought
You would never desire
You desire

I watch the night from my bedroom
The storm breaks over Capanawalla
The light flickers returns and dies

Another night another storm
Warmth of the fire alone

I can't recall what I believe
Constituted
The idea of love

In our mouths dead roses
And the language of longing

Her left pulse
Her curious tone
In passion

Every night I lay on her bed
And stroked her hair
Until my arm ached

One day
To abandon myself

Driving again in metronomic rain
To sit and listen to my mother's
Fading suite

It's only shit
In lax intimacy
I sponge

From what was once harbour   home   I think of what
    I might take
A cutting of Japonica   the piano drifted from tune
The painting of the boat in full sail at the prow of the stairs

Today I did not taste earth
Touch a woman
Or call out in despair

Any day now
We will discover how to live
There will be time for affection

Printed in the United Kingdom
by Lightning Source UK Ltd.
126538UK00001B/148-264/P